WHY
SIEUR
DE LA SALLE
MATTERS TO TEXAS

By Lynn Peppas

Published in 2014 by The Rosen Publishing Group, Inc.
29 East 21st Street, New York, NY 10010

First Edition

Developed, written, and produced by Digital Discovery Publishing
Editors: Molly Aloian, Wendy Scavuzzo
Design & Production: Katherine Berti
Photo research: Crystal Sikkens, Allison Napier
Proofreader: Sarah Cairns

Photo Credits: American Antiquarian Society, Worcester, Massachusetts, USA / The Bridgeman Art Library: 8 (bottom)
Chateau de Versailles, France / Giraudon / The Bridgeman Art Library: 16
Gianni Dagli Orti/The Art Archive at Art Resource, NY: 18
Gilcrease Museum: 15
The Granger Collection, New York: 4, 9, 10, 12, 13, 27 (top)
NASA/Wikimedia Commons: 14 (top right)
New York Public Library: 23, 24
Shutterstock: 5, 6, 14 (middle), 17, 20 (top), 22
Texas Historical Commission: 26, 28, 29, 30 (left)
Texas Shores Magazine: 15 (bottom)
Wikimedia Commons: cover, 1, 13, 14 (top left), 27 (bottom)
Maps by Digital Discovery Publishing: 5, 6, 7 (bottom), 11, 15 (top), 20 (top), 22

All websites were live and accurate at the time of printing.

Library of Congress Cataloging-in-Publication Data

Peppas, Lynn.
Why Sieur de la Salle matters to Texas / by Lynn Peppas.
  p. cm. – (Texas perspectives)
Includes index.
ISBN 978-1-4777-0917-7 (library binding)Digital Discovery Publishing – ISBN 978-1-4777-0943-6 (pbk.) – ISBN 978-1-4777-0944-3
  (6-pack)
1. La Salle, Robert Cavelier, sieur de, 1643-1687 – Juvenile literature. 2. North America – Discovery and exploration – French – Juvenile literature. 3. Mississippi River Valley – Discovery and exploration – French – Juvenile literature. I. Peppas, Lynn. II. Title.
F1030.5 P47 2013
976.4–dc23

Manufactured in the United States of America

CPSIA Compliance Information: Batch W13PK: For Further Information contact Rosen Publishing, New York, New York at 1-800-237-9932

CONTENTS

AMBUSHED!

In March 1687, the French explorer René-Robert Cavelier, who was better known as Sieur de La Salle, went searching for six fellow explorers who were missing. The men had strayed from the main group traveling through the wilderness of Texas. A **friar** named Anastase Douay and an Indian guide went with La Salle to help with the search. Before he left camp, La Salle talked to his loyal friend Henri Joutel. La Salle asked Joutel if the missing men were plotting against him. Joutel assured him that he had heard nothing.

Henri Joutel explains his discussion with La Salle in the book *The Pioneers of France in the New World,* published in 1865:

> *That evening, while we were talking about what could have happened to the absent men, [La Salle] seemed to have a [suspicion] of what was to take place. He asked me if I had heard of any [plotting] against them....I answered that I had heard nothing.*

INTO A TRAP

Finally, La Salle, the friar, and their Indian guide found the campsite of the missing men. La Salle was relieved that the search was over. La Salle fired shots into the air to let the missing men know he was nearby. One of the missing men appeared and spoke rudely to La Salle. La Salle became angry and began to chase the man. La Salle did not know it, but he was running into a dangerous trap that was going to cost him his life.

▼ *René-Robert Cavelier, was also known as Sieur de La Salle. During the 1600s in France, it was the custom to call a man from a wealthy family "sieur," which means "sir" in English.*

Two other men were lying in the grass with their guns, ready to shoot La Salle. Each man fired, and one of the shots hit La Salle in the head. He fell down, dead. When La Salle died, so did France's dream of colonizing what is now Texas.

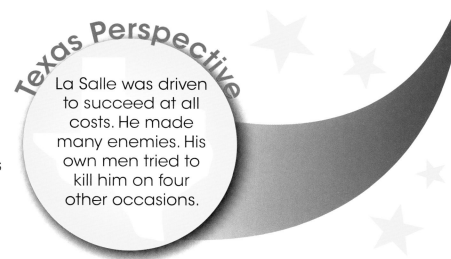

SIEUR DE LA SALLE'S TEXAS

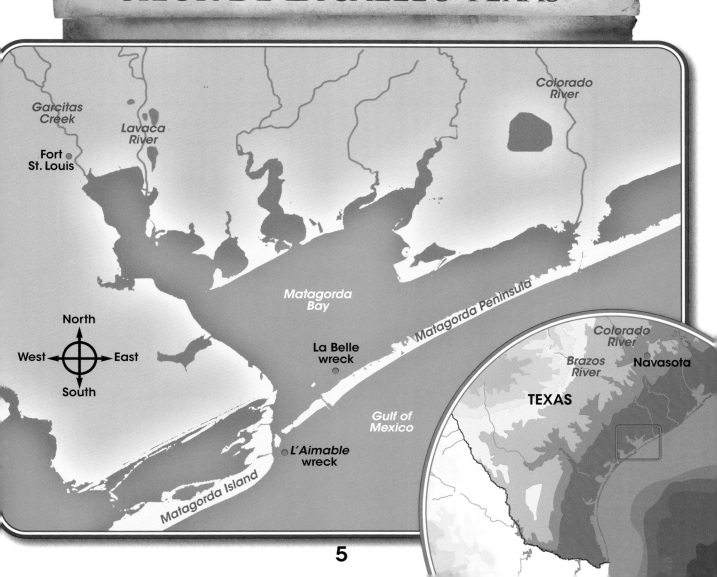

Garcitas Creek

Lavaca River

Colorado River

Fort St. Louis

North
West — East
South

Matagorda Bay

Matagorda Peninsula

La Belle wreck

Gulf of Mexico

L'Aimable wreck

Matagorda Island

Colorado River

Brazos River

Navasota

TEXAS

EARLY LIFE

René-Robert Cavelier was born in November 1643 in Rouen, France. His father, Jean, was a rich **merchant,** and his family lived on an estate called La Salle. Although he had five brothers and sisters, René-Robert's father gave the family estate to him. After that, he became known as Sieur de La Salle.

MONTREAL BOUND

La Salle was a good student and did especially well in mathematics and the sciences. After his father died, La Salle moved to Montreal, Canada, in 1666. His older brother, a priest named Abbé Jean Cavelier, lived in Montreal, too. There were many groups of Indians, including the Iroquois, living in Montreal. La Salle learned to speak different Indian languages.

La Salle was 23 when he made the journey by boat from his home in France to Montreal, Canada. He later traveled to Texas.

EXPLORER'S DREAMS

La Salle, like other early European explorers, dreamed of finding a waterway from Europe to China. This route was called the Northwest Passage. During his time in Montreal, La Salle explored other areas of North America looking for the Northwest Passage.

The Indians he met told him about a great river that lay to the west. La Salle decided to explore the Great Lakes area in search of the river. After he traveled down the St. Lawrence River, he built Fort Frontenac and a trading post at Lake Ontario. King Louis XIV of France was happy with La Salle's exploration and work. The king gave Fort Frontenac to La Salle and wanted him to begin more **colonies** in North America.

▲
In 1673, La Salle built a fort at what is now Kingston, Ontario. It became an important trading post and military base called Fort Frontenac.

NORTHWEST PASSAGE

Many European explorers in the 1500s and 1600s searched for a waterway from Europe to China. China had valuable trade goods such as silk and spices that the Europeans wanted. The overland trade route from Europe to China was dangerous and expensive to cross, though. Although the waterway that connected the Atlantic and Pacific oceans had not yet been discovered, it was called the Northwest Passage.

SOUTH TO THE MISSISSIPPI

In late 1678, La Salle left Fort Frontenac to explore the Great Lakes. He then sent his ship back to Fort Frontenac and traveled south on foot with some of his men along the St. Joseph, Kankakee, and Illinois rivers. Along the Illinois River, the men built another fort called Fort Heartbreak. La Salle traveled back to Fort Frontenac, then returned south once again until he reached the Mississippi River. He and his men built another fort called Fort Prudhomme near the area known today as Memphis, Tennessee.

TEXAS BEFORE LA SALLE

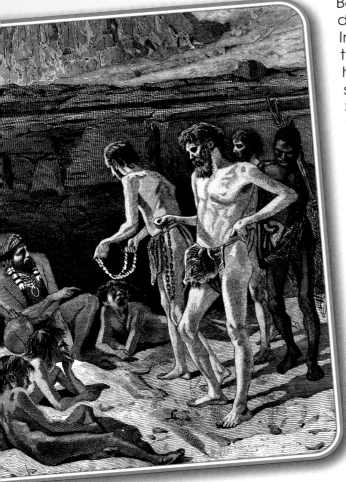

Before La Salle arrived in Texas in 1685, different groups of Indians lived in the area. Indians had been living in Texas for thousands of years. Most were **nomadic** hunters and gatherers. They had never seen explorers from Europe before La Salle. Some Indians in Texas may have heard their **ancestors** tell stories about a Spanish explorer named Álvar Núñez Cabeza de Vaca. For many years, Cabeza de Vaca had lived among different southern groups of Texas Indians. The Indians may have also heard stories about the Spanish living in New Spain, which is the present-day country of Mexico.

◀ *The Spanish explorer Álvar Núñez Cabeza de Vaca was the first European to visit Texas. He was stranded there with a few other men more than 100 years before La Salle arrived. Before he was rescued, Cabeza de Vaca spent time trading goods with local groups of Indians.*

8

CLAIMED FOR FRANCE

In 1682, La Salle led the first European **expedition** down the Mississippi River to the mouth of the Gulf of Mexico. He claimed the land for France and named it Louisiana, after King Louis XIV. Even though he had not found the Northwest Passage, La Salle knew his discovery would still mean a great deal to the king. La Salle hoped to build a trading post and fort at the mouth of the Mississippi River, but the French governor of Quebec would not support La Salle's idea. La Salle decided to sail to France and talk to the king.

Texas Perspective

Indians living on the Gulf Coast of Texas had never seen a European before La Salle arrived in the 1680s.

When La Salle claimed the entire Mississippi region for France on April 9, 1682, it included all the lands, resources, and peoples in the area. This turned out to be about one-half of the entire continent of North America!

3 LAND FOR FRANCE

La Salle sailed back to France to talk to the king about his plans to start a French colony near the mouth of the Mississippi River and the Gulf of Mexico. La Salle's plan was welcomed by King Louis XIV, who wanted France to claim land in the New World.

A NEW COLONY

At the time, King Louis was angry that the Spanish would not let the French enter the Gulf of Mexico. A French port on the Gulf of Mexico would open up opportunities for the French to claim land and establish new colonies. It would also help the French overtake the **sparsely** populated Spanish provinces, such as New Biscay, where there were valuable silver mines. The French also wanted to **convert** Indians to Christianity. To start a new colony, King Louis granted La Salle two ships, some cannons, and 300 colonists, including men, women, and children.

King Louis XIV granted La Salle only two ships for his voyage. La Salle had to arrange for two more ships himself.

From the last letter La Salle wrote to his mother before setting sail for the Mississippi River, July 18, 1684:

At last, after having waited a long time for a favorable wind, and having had a great many difficulties to overcome, we are setting sail with four vessels, and nearly 400 men on board....We are not going by way of Canada, but by the Gulf of Mexico.

TROUBLE ON BOARD

King Louis put a royal navy captain named Tanneguy le Gallois de Beaujeu in charge of the expedition. The expedition left France on July 24, 1684. La Salle was not happy because he wanted to be in charge at sea and on land. He and Beaujeu fought often during the voyage.

After two months, the ships came to the Caribbean island of Santo Domingo. La Salle planned to land at Port-de-Paix. Beaujeu refused and led the ships to anchor at the other side of the island. One of the ships, the *Saint François*, was carrying food, tools, and other items needed for the colony. The ship was captured by Spanish pirates. La Salle was furious and he blamed Beaujeu for the loss.

COLONIZING NORTH AMERICA

When La Salle arrived at Montreal in 1666, other Europeans had already settled and colonized different areas of North America. The Spanish arrived in the late 1500s. They colonized areas in South and Central America, as well as parts of North America known today as Mexico and the states of New Mexico and Texas. The area became known as New Spain. In the early 1600s, the British settled in areas farther north and along the Atlantic coast of North America. The French arrived in Canada in the early 1600s. They settled farther north in present-day Quebec.

The Spanish, who settled in New Spain, claimed lands in Texas and Florida, but did not have colonies in place to defend the area. They worried the French would move in and take over their lands. The Spanish wanted complete control over the Gulf of Mexico. ►

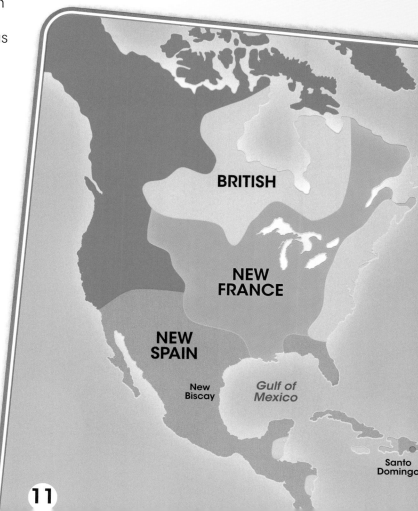

BRITISH

NEW FRANCE

NEW SPAIN

New Biscay

Gulf of Mexico

Santo Domingo

TROPICAL FEVER

While exploring Santo Domingo, La Salle became ill with a fever. La Salle's brother, Jean, cared for him on the island. Many men on the expedition disliked La Salle and hoped he would not recover from his illness. Several other men caught diseases, and some died.

LOST IN A GULF

It took months for La Salle to recover from his illness. On November 25, 1684, the expedition finally left for the mouth of the Mississippi River. After nearly a month of searching, they spotted the Gulf of Mexico on December 28. The ships' pilots were unfamiliar with the area. They thought they were near the Mississippi River, but they had passed it. They were actually on the Texas coast. They continued to search for the mouth of the Mississippi, but they argued more than ever about its whereabouts. Food and water **rations** were getting low, which made the situation even more tense.

La Salle thought he had sailed to the Mississippi River, but he had passed it. He had landed in Matagorda Bay, Texas, about 400 miles (644 km) away!

CAPSIZED IN THE BAY

In February 1685, La Salle sent a small group of men onto the shore of Matagorda Island. One of the men believed they had found the mouth of the Mississippi River, but it was actually Matagorda Bay. When La Salle and his men were onshore making a canoe, a group of Karankawa Indians kidnapped some of the men. La Salle negotiated with the Karankawa and the men were returned peacefully.

When La Salle was at the Indian campsite, he heard a ship's cannon blast. He returned to find that the ship *L'Aimable* had **capsized** on a sandbar. La Salle and his men tried to save what little cargo they could, such as gunpowder and flour. Indians also tried to gather treasures from the capsized ship, but La Salle's men protected their provisions.

This photo shows part of Matagorda Bay as it looks today.

THE TEXAS LANDSCAPE

The southwest coast of Texas along the Gulf of Mexico has flat grasslands, sandy dunes, and marshes. There are also some wooded areas along streams that run into Matagorda Bay. It is a semiarid region, which means there is little rainfall. On average, the area receives 40 to 60 inches (102–152 cm) of rain every year. During the summer, it is hot and humid with temperatures reaching up to 96° F (36° C). Winters are usually mild.

◄ ▼ *La Salle and his colonists encountered many birds when they landed in Texas, including spoonbills (left) and cranes (below).*

La Salle's two ships, L'Aimable *and* La Belle, *landed at Matagorda Bay, which is a large estuary. Estuaries are waterways where the salt water from seas or oceans meets freshwater from streams and rivers.*

NOT WELCOME

The Karankawa were intent on keeping the French colonists away from their traditional land. A few days after the arrival of the colonists, the Karankawa lit the nearby **prairie** on fire. The colonists saw the fire spreading quickly toward them. La Salle ordered his men to remove large patches of grass around their campsite so the fire would not engulf their camp. While the colonists were distracted, the Karankawa took some of their blankets and other belongings. Shortly after, a small party of La Salle's men went to the Karankawa campsite to retrieve the stolen items. The colonists took some of the Karankawa's canoes instead. Small and frequent **skirmishes** broke out between the two groups and usually ended in one or more deaths.

KARANKAWA

The Karankawa were the first Indians that La Salle and the colonists encountered in Texas. The Karankawa lived on the southwest Gulf coast of Texas. There were about five different groups, or bands, of Karankawa, including the Korenkake, Clamcoets, and Carancahua, living in the area. In the early 1500s, the Spanish explorer Cabeza de Vaca described the Karankawa men as being tall and physically fit, while women were shorter and stouter. Most were excellent swimmers. They decorated their bodies with tattoos, piercings, and paint.

The Karankawa lived along the Texas coast until the mid-1800s. War, loss of territory, and diseases brought by Europeans eventually caused the Karankawa to become extinct.

4

FORT ST. LOUIS

Over the next few months, La Salle's colonists were overcome by hardships and were slowly losing hope. They were ill, tired, and homesick. By the end of the summer, more than **30** settlers had died. La Salle's dream of starting a new colony and taking over nearby Spanish colonies was starting to seem impossible.

A JOLY RIDE HOME

Tanneguy le Gallois de Beaujeu returned to France on board the *Joly* in March 1685. The *Joly* was a 36-gun **man-of-war** ship. Beaujeu desperately needed food and supplies for his men. Before his departure, La Salle asked to have some cannons and iron from the ship. Beaujeu refused to take the items off his ship. He feared it would cause the *Joly* to capsize. Some of the colonists returned to France with Beaujeu. They were homesick and wished they had never left France.

Beaujeu and some of the homesick colonists returned to France on the ship Joly, *leaving La Salle in North America to continue exploring.*

FORT LIFE

La Salle found a location to settle the women, children, and most of the remaining men. It was on Garcitas Creek. La Salle named the new colony Fort St. Louis. The fort was located about 6 miles (9.7 km) from the mouth of the Lavaca River. About 34 colonists lived there, including three priests and some women and children from France. The colonists set up a few buildings and tended animals they brought from France, such as pigs, chickens, and goats. They also tried to grow some food, but a **drought** that summer killed the crops. The men hunted buffalo, deer, rabbits, and geese near the colony. Nearby water sources, such as the river and bay, also provided fish, oysters, and turtles for food.

La Salle saw so many buffalo drinking from the banks of Garcitas Creek that he called it "Rivière aux Boeufs," or "Cattle River."

In the excerpt below, La Salle's friend Henri Joutel describes life at Fort St. Louis:

> *The settlement was… on a small rise from which one could see a long distance. Toward the west and the southwest there was a prairie, very level, that continued beyond our view. Beautiful, good grasses grow here serving as [food] to an infinite number of bison.*

La Salle's attempts to find the Mississippi proved unsuccessful.

THE MISSING MISSISSIPPI

La Salle continued to explore the coast of Texas for the mouth of the Mississippi River. He left on an expedition in November 1685 with a small party of men but was unsuccessful. On April 22, 1686, La Salle and about 20 men, including his brother Jean, set out once again to search for the Mississippi River and travel up to Canada. La Salle planned to bring back provisions for the new colony but did not succeed. In fact, he returned a short time later with only eight men. Some men were believed to have run away to live with the friendly Caddo Indians. Others died during the trip.

NO WAY HOME

While La Salle was away, *La Belle* was shipwrecked and all the passengers drowned or were later killed by the Karankawa. *La Belle* carried ammunition and tools for the colony, as well as La Salle's personal papers. The loss of the ship left the colonists with no way to return to France or to get to the Mississippi River when, or if, it was ever found. The situation seemed worse than ever.

WARM WELCOME

During La Salle's travels, the expedition came across many different Indian tribes. One tribe, called the Caddo, was particularly welcoming to La Salle and his men as they traveled northeast through Texas. La Salle and his men referred to those they met from this tribe as "Cenis," but historians think they were the Hasinai band from the Caddo tribe.

Father Anastase Douay writes of his experiences with the Caddo Indians during La Salle's expedition in 1687:

> *...the women...washed our head and feet with warm water, and then placed us on a platform covered with a very neat, white mat; then followed banquets, ...dances, and other public rejoicings, day and night.*

The Caddo had permanent homes because they were farmers and did not have to travel to find food.

THE CADDO

The Caddo lived along the coastal plain. They were farmers who grew crops such as corn, squash, beans, and sunflowers. They also hunted deer, buffalo, small birds, and fish. It is believed that the Caddo learned to ride horses from the Spanish. Riding horses made hunting buffalo easier and faster. The Caddo lived in a hilly area with rich soils that supported small forests of pines and hardwood trees. Valleys were especially good for growing crops. Caddo men and women tattooed themselves by puncturing their skin with sharp, pointed objects and running charcoal over the top to dye their skin. They also painted their faces and bodies during special ceremonies and for war. They wore clothing made of animal skins decorated with seeds, feathers, and paint.

The Caddo built large grass houses that looked like giant beehives. The houses were made from log frames and covered with woven grass mats. About eight to ten people lived in each home.

La Salle returned to the fort to find that the colonists wanted to return to France. More than half of them had died and many others were sick.

BACK AT THE FORT

Shortly after leaving the Caddo, La Salle fell ill for months. The party decided to go back to Fort St. Louis with horses they had received from the Caddo. The remaining colonists at the fort were tired of harsh weather, no permanent homes, worn-out clothing, and living in constant fear of Indian attacks. It was not a lifestyle they were used to, and some were angry with La Salle. They felt he had promised them a much more successful and comfortable life. With no ships to take them to France, though, La Salle decided on a new plan. They would travel on land to Canada.

5

ASSASSINATION!

In January 1687, La Salle's final expedition to Canada set out. La Salle and many of his men were exhausted, starving, and sick, but they pushed themselves to carry on. La Salle's good-bye speech to the colonists at Fort St. Louis was the last time they saw him.

FROM TEXAS TO CANADA

La Salle's plan for the expedition was to travel north across Texas to Canada. Once they reached Quebec, Canada, La Salle planned to send his brother, Jean, and some other colonists on a ship to France. About 20 colonists remained behind at Fort St. Louis.

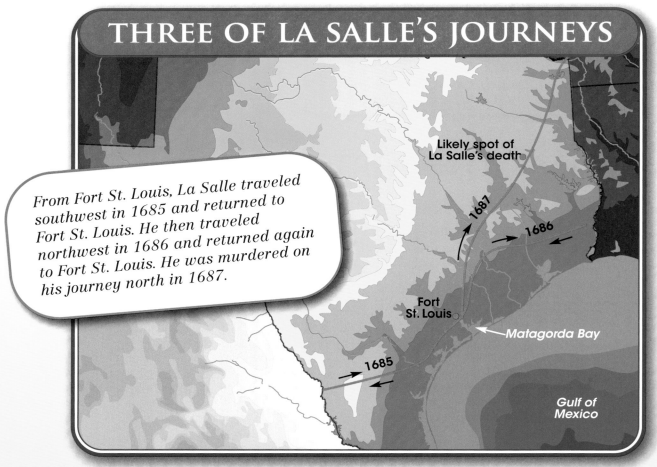

THREE OF LA SALLE'S JOURNEYS

From Fort St. Louis, La Salle traveled southwest in 1685 and returned to Fort St. Louis. He then traveled northwest in 1686 and returned again to Fort St. Louis. He was murdered on his journey north in 1687.

Likely spot of La Salle's death

1687

1686

Fort St. Louis

Matagorda Bay

1685

Gulf of Mexico

The five horses La Salle had acquired from the Caddo were used to carry supplies.

DIFFICULT AND DANGEROUS

La Salle and his men had no roads or pathways to guide them through the Texas wilderness. It was a difficult and dangerous journey. The men did not have proper shoes. They wore **moccasins** made from animal skins. La Salle's men made a boat from buffalo skins to help them travel across waterways, such as the Colorado River, Brazos River, and many streams. They had no shelter to protect them from stormy weather, so they built **makeshift** huts of bark and grasses. At night, one man always remained on the lookout for thieves or attackers. The men on the expedition were miserable.

MARCH MURDERS

In mid-March, La Salle sent out a small party of seven men, including his servant, Saget, and his friend, Nika, who was a hunter. The men were sent to look for food they had hidden on a previous expedition. The food had rotted, though, so Nika shot two buffalo. Saget went to bring back horses to carry the buffalo meat. He returned with the horses and two men, including Moranget, who was not well liked. Moranget became angry and tried to take the meat for himself.

Five of the men made plans to murder Moranget, Nika, and Saget that night. They killed the men with an ax while they slept. The murderers then plotted to kill La Salle.

LA SALLE WORRIES

La Salle became suspicious when all the members of the hunting party did not return. He asked an Indian guide to help him find the missing men. The night before he left, La Salle asked his friend Henri Joutel whether he had heard that the others in the hunting party were angry with him.

▶ *La Salle worried his men were plotting against him.*

In the excerpt below, La Salle's friend Henri Joutel recalls his conversation with La Salle the evening before La Salle left to find the missing members of the hunting party:

[La Salle] asked me if I had heard of the men [planning] something among themselves, or if I had noticed that they had some evil plot. I said that I had not heard anything...Furthermore, as they were convinced that I would defend [La Salle's] interests, they would not have told me if they had some wicked design.

SHOT DEAD

La Salle set out to find the men with his Indian guide and a friar named Anastase Douay. On March 19, 1687, the missing men ambushed La Salle. Some hid behind nearby trees and long grasses with their guns, while one man stood where La Salle could easily spot him. La Salle called out to him, asking where the others were. The man shouted rudely at La Salle. La Salle walked toward the man and, as he did, the men lying in the grass shot him. The shot from Pierre Duhaut killed La Salle. The men did not murder the friar or the guide.

Texas Perspective

Of the almost 200 colonists La Salle brought to Texas, only 15 remained alive to tell their story five years later.

AFTER LA SALLE'S ASSASSINATION

The next year, the 20 remaining people living at Fort St. Louis were attacked by a group of Karankawa warriors. The Karankawa killed everyone in the colony except for five children, whom they took back with them. The Spanish had been searching for La Salle's colony for almost four years. Spanish General Alonso de León and his men finally found the ruined colony in April 1689. They burned it to the ground and buried eight cannons. The Spanish later found the missing children living with Indians. The Spanish took the children with them to Mexico.

La Salle was 43 years old when he was assassinated north of the Brazos River in Texas.

LA SALLE'S LEGACY

Before Sieur de La Salle arrived on the Gulf shore of Texas in February 1685, there were no Europeans living in Texas. The Spanish living in Mexico claimed Texas as part of New Spain but had not established forts or colonies in the area. La Salle was the very first European to attempt to establish a colony in the untamed and unfamiliar wilderness. The colony was a failure, but La Salle will always be remembered as the leader of the first real exploration of the Texas Gulf Coast.

FAILED FRENCH PLANS

▲ *The Spanish built Presidio la Bahia in 1721 on the ruins of Fort St. Louis. It was one of the earliest Spanish presidios, or forts, in Texas.*

When La Salle and his crew arrived on the shores of Texas, they did so in secrecy. King Louis XIV of France wanted to take advantage of La Salle's colony as a way to overtake small Spanish mining settlements and take control of the Gulf of Mexico. The French would also benefit by gaining control of the areas inland along the Mississippi River, which stretches in a north and south direction through most of the United States and drains into the Gulf of Mexico.

From La Salle's friend Henri Joutel:

[La Salle's] firmness, his courage, his great knowledge of the arts and sciences...and his untiring energy...would have won at last a glorious success for his grand enterprise, had not all his fine qualities been counterbalanced by a [snobbishness]...and by a harshness toward those under his command, which drew upon him a...hatred, and was at last the cause of his death.

SPANISH INTEREST

La Salle's arrival in Texas triggered a growing European interest in exploring and colonizing the land, not only for the French, but also for the Spanish. The Spanish were upset when they heard the French were forming a colony near the Gulf of Mexico, so they began to colonize parts of Texas to protect their claim to the land. The Spanish built missions and forts in Texas after hearing about the French colony of Fort St. Louis.

Years later, in 1803, when the French sold their claimed land of "Louisiana" to the United States, portions of northern Texas were included because of La Salle's earlier explorations.

LA SALLE, TEXAS

La Salle's name and legacy live on in a county that was named after him in the state of Texas. La Salle County was officially formed in 1858 and is located in south Texas.

◄ *This statue of La Salle is located in Navasota, Texas, near where La Salle was killed.*

27

RAISING LA BELLE

One of the ships from La Salle's famous journey to Texas, *La Belle*, sunk in 1687 in Matagorda Bay. It remained there for more than 300 years. In 1995, a crew of archaeologists from the Texas Historical Commission discovered a cannon on board the ship. In 1996, the shipwreck was raised at a cost of more than $2 million.

It took more than nine months to bring the ship and its contents to the surface. The ship was surrounded by mud, which helped to preserve it and most of the artifacts aboard. Artifacts, such as tools, weapons, dishes, glass beads, cannons, rope, and a variety of other items, were discovered, and carefully cleaned and preserved. More than one million artifacts were found on *La Belle*.

Many of the artifacts found on La Belle *are on display in museums throughout Texas.*

SHARED TREASURES

The French government claimed the ship and its contents as theirs, according to a law that says a sunken ship belongs to the country from which it came. In 2003, the Texas Historical Commission and the French government decided that the French did, in fact, own *La Belle* and its contents, but that the Texas Historical Commission would be allowed to care for and show it in the United States.

From Barto Arnold, team leader from the Texas Historical Commission working on *La Belle*:

" La Salle comes alive again. I feel as though I'm reaching across 300 years to shake his hand. "

A burial site was uncovered by archaeologists in Fort St. Louis. The skeletons are believed to be the three colonists who were killed by the Karankawa and later buried by the Spanish.

FORT ST. LOUIS

The exact location of Fort St. Louis had been a mystery for years. Archaeologists had been searching for clues to the whereabouts of Fort St. Louis at a ranch in Victoria County owned by Claude Keeran. In 1996, a ranch worker found a small part of a cannon buried underground. Archaeologists from the Texas Historical Commission discovered the remaining eight cannons buried near the first.

◄ *French cannons uncovered on a private ranch in Victoria County finally confirmed the location of Fort St. Louis. Seven of the cannons can be seen at the Museum of the Coastal Bend, in Victoria County, Texas.*

A
JOURNAL
Of the LAST
VOYAGE
Perform'd by
Monfr. de la Sale,
TO THE
GULPH of MEXICO,
To find out the
Mouth of the *Miffifipi* River;
CONTAINING,
An Account of the Settlements he endeavour'd to make on the Coaft of the aforefaid *Bay*, his unfortunate Death, and the Travels of his Companions for the Space of Eight Hundred Leagues across that Inland Country of *America*, now call'd *Louifiana*, (and given by the King of *France* to M. *Crozat*,)till they came into *Canada*.

Written in French *by Monfieur* JOUTEL, *A Commander in that Expedition*; *And Tranflated from the Edition juft publifh'd at* Paris.

With an exaft Map of that vaft Country,and a Copy of the *Letters Patents* granted by the K.of *France* to M. *Crozat*.

LONDON, Printed for *A. Bell* at the *Crofs-Keys* and *Bible* in *Cornhill*, B. *Lintott* at the *Crofs Keys* in Fleet-ftreet, and *J. Baker* in *Pater-Nofter-Row*, 1714.

▲ *Henri Joutel's journal of La Salle's expedition in Texas was first published in English in 1714.*

LEARNING MORE

BOOKS

Roza, Greg, *Early Explorers of Texas*. Spotlight on Texas. New York: Rosen Publishing, 2010.

Zronik, John Paul, *Sieur de La Salle: New World Adventurer*. New York: Crabtree Publishing, 2006.

HISTORIC SITES

The Texas Maritime Museum: Exhibit: The La Salle Odyssey,
www.texasmaritimemuseum.org/ lasalle_odyssey.html

WEBSITES @

Corpus Christi Museum of Science and History: The French in Texas
www.ccmuseumedres.com/french.htm

NOVA Online – Voyage of Doom
www.pbs.org/nova/lasalle

Texas Beyond History: Fort St. Louis
www.texasbeyondhistory.net/stlouis/index.html

Texas Beyond History – *La Belle*
www.texasbeyondhistory.net/belle/index.html

TIMELINE

Texas | Sieur de La Salle

1500s–1600s Europeans sail across the Atlantic Ocean and settle in eastern parts of North America.

1643 René-Robert Cavelier, known as Sieur de La Salle, is born on November 21 in Rouen, France.

1666 Sails from France to Montreal, Quebec, Canada.

1673 Builds Fort Frontenac near the mouth of the St. Lawrence River and Lake Ontario, in Canada.

1682 Travels the Mississippi River by ship to the Gulf of Mexico; claims Louisiana for France.

1684 Arrives in France to convince the king to help put together an expedition to build a French colony in Louisiana; expedition leaves France and sails to North America; lands too far west on coastal shore of Texas near Matagorda Bay.

1685 Continues to search for mouth of Mississippi River; fighting occurs between Indians and French settlers; the ship *L'Aimable* is shipwrecked; encounters Karankawa Indians; another ship, *Joly*, returns to France; new settlement called Fort St. Louis is made.

1686 Leads new party to explore coast of Texas and find mouth of the Mississippi River; the last ship of the expedition, *La Belle*, sinks in Matagorda Bay; encounters Caddo Indians.

1687 Sets out on expedition to Canada around January 7; murdered by members of his own crew on March 19.

1689 Spanish General Alonso de León and his men find the ruined colony of Fort St. Louis in April.

1803 The Louisiana Purchase, the sale of Louisiana by the French to the Americans, includes portions of Texas because of La Salle's explorations.

1858 A county in the state of Texas is named La Salle after the French explorer.

1996 The ship *La Belle* is raised from Matagorda Bay; artifacts such as cannons, weapons, and dishes are preserved and given to the Texas Historical Commission; archaeologists find eight cannons and locate Fort St. Louis.

GLOSSARY

ancestors (AN-ses-terz) Relatives who lived long ago.

capsized (KAP-syzd) Became overturned.

colonies (KAH-luh-neez) New places where people move that are still ruled by the leaders of the country from which they came.

convert (kun-VERT) To change from one faith to another.

drought (DROWT) A period of dryness that causes harm to crops.

expedition (ek-spuh-DIH-shun) A trip for a special purpose.

friar (FRY-ur) A brother in a communal religious order. Friars can be priests.

makeshift (MAYK-shift) Crude, or simple, and temporary.

man-of-war (ma-nuv-WOR) A warship of a recognized navy.

merchant (MER-chunt) Someone who owns a business that sells goods.

moccasins (MAH-kuh-sinz) Native American shoes made of leather and often decorated with beads.

nomadic (noh-MA-dik) Roaming about from place to place.

prairie (PRER-ee) A large area of flat land with grass but few or no trees.

rations (RA-shunz) Food given to people in controlled amounts so that it will last for a certain amount of time.

skirmishes (SKUR-mish-ez) Brief fights or encounters.

sparsely (SPAHRS-lee) Describing something that is few in number and very spread out.

INDEX